The Old Ambassador and Other Poems

Wayne Courtois

Spartan
Press

Spartan Press
Kansas City, Missouri
spartanpresskc.com

Spartan
Press

Acknowledgments:

Special Thanks to Jason Ryberg, Maryfrances Wagner, Catherine Anderson, Robin Wayne Bailey, Joel Barrett, James Benger, Shawn Pavey

"When It Comes" first appeared, in different form, in the anthology The Shining Years, ed. by Gary Lechliter (Blue Wild Indigo Productions, 2020).

TABLE OF CONTENTS

For Ralph—

Forever part
of the journey

There is no intensity of love or feeling that does not involve the risk of crippling hurt. It is a duty to take this risk, to love and feel without defense or reserve.

- William S. Burroughs

The Old Ambassador
and Other Poems

When It Comes

How will it happen, when it comes?
Will we be together?
Will there be warning enough?

Will it all go in one swipe,
like an eraser across a chalkboard
back when there were chalkboards?

I remember clapping erasers after school,
outside, in the cold, yellow and white dust rising.
Sometimes it felt good to hit things together.

Later on other things felt good,
but we felt bad about them. In time,
we joined the ranks of a despised minority.

When it seems we've been despised long enough,
someone else gets knifed or shot, set on fire,
beaten to death, torn limb from limb.

How will it happen, when it comes?
Will everyone have suffered enough
So you and I can lie side by side,

Holding hands when it comes?

Plain Rooms

What if we're wrong?
What if we're meant
to fight this pull

strong as gravity?
Suppose our search
for love is, in the

end, just depravity?
What if those sour,
condemning faces are

right, and we are only
manifestations of
the night, creeping

grave to grave, life
too good for
the likes of us—

the life of others,
with its sweet, safe
passage to grace?

What did we want?
Remind me, will
you? Christ, were

we meant to kill you?
God? Was that you
I saw the other day,

at that church on
Broadway? A skinny
old man with a cupful

of pencils, shaking
down the soup line
for spare change?

The derelicts laughed,
called you deranged.
"'Bout time," someone

muttered. "'Bout time
God lost his mind."
For me, madness

would be a luxury.
I know too well
my stake is whatever

I'm allowed to take,
my end pre-ordained,
a bed to lie on,

stripped and stained,
the afterlife whatever
I can keep pretending.

Only the hooker down
the hall guarantees
a happy ending.

As for you and me,
my love, didn't we
meet in a plain room

like this, reeking of
piss, cigarettes, and
beer? What say we

get out of here, find
another plain room,
with a prairie view.

We'll hold hands,
watch the sun set,
and never forget

we love each other.
If this life is a bargain
made in the dark,

out of ignorance and
sin, then come to me.
Let damnation begin.

Heteronormative Bar-B-Q Sandwich

They stand in front of us in line,
waiting to get to the register
to order barbecue and beer.
Wrapped around each other
like parts of a pretzel,
she jams one hand in his hip
pocket, and he returns the favor.

In the half-light from the bar
they gaze into each other's eyes
and smile and peck at each
other like little birds.

You and I stand, my right hand
barely brushing your left.
Conscious of the crowd,
we peer around. *Nothing*
to see here, folks,
just a couple of dudes
getting barbecue and beer.

Now He and She
are twined even tighter,
as close as two bodies can get
without making a baby.
And that will be happening
soon—any minute.

"They're gonna *do it*," I whisper.
"Shut *up*," you whisper.

Someday they'll shake their heads
over what we had to go through,
how careful we had to be,
never seeming to claim
a place at the table.

But let the record show
gays were killed for this:
a beer and a barbecue sandwich
at the wrong time in the wrong place.
More than any straight couple
about to fuck on the bar floor,
we knew the cost of loving.

Incident on 18th Street

Outside my office building,
swiping my ID card,
not getting in.

Coming from nowhere
stick man in a parka,
grabbing my wrist,
trying to get my computer bag.

Tighten my grip, try to yell.
Two of us breathing hard.
Nostrils steaming.

"Come on, man.
Gimme me that goddamn thing.
What you care?
You got your shit backed up, ain'tcha?"

Jaw unlocking. "Look, asshole.
There's no *backup*. There's *nothing*.
Just *this moment, right now*. This is *it*."

His hand dropping, empty.

Gone faster than he came,

Running like hell down the street.

Queer Time of Day

The sun is setting.
Too soon for headlights.
I put my sunglass clips on,
take them off, put them on.

I see you, the you
I'm driving toward,
you on the sofa
with the cat on your lap,

and I'm that close
to honking at the SUV
that keeps crossing into my
lane, then slowing down.

On Main Street, two lanes
closed for no apparent
reason. I want to strangle
somebody, but I've got

a new rule against getting
angry on the drive
to and from work. Instead,
I breathe. Clear my head

of thoughts—disturbingly
easy to do. I coast,
letting gravity do
the work of stopping

at a red light. Two more
lanes to watch out for ahead:
one that's often closed,
and one lane drivers can't

resist illegally parking in.
If you get stuck behind a
parked car, forget about ever
seeing your loved ones again.

This time I avoid the trap.
I think of you again, always,
in this queer time of day,
when commuters sort

themselves out, the straight
and the gay, the blessed
and the sinners, journeying
home to lookalike dinners.

The Master

The certainty scorches my brain:
I will never, ever be as good
as this one or that one, or
him, or her, or them.

Never be read till the lights
go out in freshman dorms,
never discussed in poetry
workshops or dissertations,

never invited to read on campus,
never stalked by a student.
Never fill the auditorium
at the library, never be sketched

by a clever artist, or asked
to sign a book, or found
by admirers obsessed with
discovering my hidden lair.

How is it I'll sit for hours
groping for words to describe
the most common things and
emotions, scratching my head

with one hand while typing l-o-v-e
with the other, stunned
by the fact that I don't seem
to know anything about

anything—and yet I have
this command, this grasp,
this mastery, this crystal-clear
knowledge of *never*.

City of No Return

I.

City of music,
why settle here,
between river and

lonesome prairie?
Was it lonesomeness
you treasured most?

Jazz took root here,
like graft. Imagine
the District decades

ago: stout black men
with their women
and cigars, wreathed

in smoke and the
most inspired
music of their time.

The future didn't
belong to them, but the
present moment,

the riff, the swing
and the backbeat,
lay at their feet.

Decades later, a black
sax player named
Steve Harvey was

beaten to death
in the shadow of
the Liberty Memorial,

south and west of
12th & Vine. Did he
even know the park

was a gay cruising area?
His killer did. He went
to prison, but only

after a gay white man,
an earlier victim who
had escaped, came

forward to testify.
A few years after that,
I moved in with

a young black man
on Campbell Street
in midtown. I had

traveled a long way
to be with him. The
first weekend he

took me to his church.
I was the only white face.
The preacher asked the

swaying congregation
for a silver offering. I
put a dollar bill

in the collection plate.
Later, in his car, my
lover was furious.

"It was supposed
to be a *silver* offering,"
he snapped. "Well,"

I snapped back, "I
didn't have any change.
Anyway, I've never

known a church
to turn down money.
So fuck you."

"Well, fuck *you*," he said.
How often we would
say those words. Also

"Kiss my ass" and "Eat
me," and "I'm from the
"Show-Me State" and

"I'm from the Blow-Me
State." We lived in
that airless space where

couples don't get along,
except when they're
touching each other.

On the night I foresaw
I'd be killed if I stayed
with him, him with

his gun and his
enemies, I said
I was leaving. He

begged me not to,
said he couldn't
live without me.

It was the first time
I ever believed
what he said.

I moved into a once-
grand apartment
house, on a cusp

between neighborhoods
Black and White. I
was walking one night

when my former lover
pulled his car up
beside me. I got in.

"I hope," he said, "you
can forgive me."
Somehow, I knew

I'd never see him
again. I hugged him.
"I forgive you, of

course I forgive you."
Years later I searched
the internet, just on

a whim, and found his
death notice. He died in 2009,
just outside St. Louis,

48 years old. I never
knew how or why.
"I forgive you": how easy

it is to offer
something as carefree
as forgiveness. After

all, God forgives,
and He stopped caring
long ago.

II.

Now, I have a decent
husband. A job. A
house. A car. I

drive it down by
the river. Not
long ago, a family

jumped off the Bond
Bridge. Mother and
father and baby,

witnesses said. The
mother held the baby
wrapped in a blanket.

Later, they said it
wasn't a mother and
father who jumped,

but a father and daughter.
It was probably her
little dog she held,

a Chihuahua mix—held
in one arm, so daughter
and father could hold

hands when they jumped.
The man's body
surfaced two months

later. The woman's
was never found.
Their names were

never released. And
the little dog was
never mentioned again.

Wrapped in a
blanket, clutched
to his mama's chest,

he may have heard
a few last heartbeats
as they fell.

To a Demon (The First Husband Rag)

Look at you, haunting the fiery pits of hell.
Great fit for you! Awesome! Not even
A social worker could have done as well.

I see you also haunting the fiery pits
Of my heart. Now, here you really
Feel at home, working the bellows

As flames grow higher and higher.
Once we knew a different kind of fire,
Lighting our days, consuming our nights.

Oh, right, it was going to last forever.
You, there, roasting my heart—
do you remember that part?

Be sure to keep a record of what you're
Doing there. Be sure to lick your fingers
And blow a chef's kiss when it's done.

I Move Slow

I move slow, tremble when I
touch things. They tremble too. A
glass skitters, orange juice slops

down the side. There is a tide
in the affairs of men that
scatters us out of reach, like

bottle caps on a beach. I
saw a young man face down on
the ground, another with his

head blown off. Parents hide their
faces in their hands. Their sons
are shot, or beaten to death,

or driven to kill themselves
to stop the pain they tried to
suffer through, but could not.

We carry them on our backs,
these dead. Their killers brush past
us, glancing at their watches.

Maybe God casts a broken
net, His last mercy not to
forgive, but forget. I move

slow, grieving for those who
waved goodbye, unaware
it was their final leaving.

The Mourning Dove

After breakfast we take our coffee
to the living room. In this urban
neighborhood formerly known
for construction and traffic noise,
the mourning dove leans on its note
like a hollowed-out car horn.

Yesterday we drove two blocks
to the park, intending to take a walk.
Ten minutes in we had to stop.
Trying to find comfort on an iron
bench: *Where is the pain coming
from? Is it your back or your hip?*

Another day, another breakfast.
The mourning dove leans on its
note. How quiet we are, listening.
And when the note stops,
how quiet we are, waiting.

Strange World

I don't recognize the faces
On the tabloids
In the check-out line.

The slightly familiar ones
Look like death masks
From a hundred years ago.

Outside, the cars in the
parking lot all look alike.
I should be able to pick one out.

The songs on the car radio
sound identical.
Surely the artists vary—don't they?

What if this strange world
Gets even smaller,
its mystery clinging to those I love?

I would know the horror
of not recognizing you, my love,
or even knowing my own home.

But oh, the ecstasy,

The unbridled joy I would feel

in no longer recognizing me.

The Old Ambassador

I.

They're tearing up Broadway for
the umpteenth, traffic's single
file Armour to Valentine.

Orange netting noses the
stone lions at Kansas
City Life Insurance. Dull

yellow digging equipment—
sitting on small wheels
with balloon tires and hubcaps—

sits idle as car horns build
to a crescendo. There's a
never-changingness about

this neighborhood, despite
the uproar—like the old
Ambassador, where I live,

looking down at that traffic.
Remember when they used to
paint doors right over the doorknob,

right over the skeleton
key in the lock, if there was
one? Have you ever grabbed a

doorknob that's been painted
over? It's like shaking hands
with a ghost. Know what it's like

to open a door that was
once painted shut? It squeaks and
rubs like something not meant to

be. Me, I've got a hall door,
closet door, bedroom door,
bathroom door. Three windows,

painted shut. I guess I'll be
painted shut someday, even
my holes. That will be it.

But clutter, now: clutter is
a living thing that will, like
the cockroach, outlast us all,

following its own laws. For
instance, the corners of a
stack of paper, once aligned,

will skew as far apart as
the planets when it's set down.
Clutter works unseen, as in

the box where jewelry gets
entangled, all by itself.
Yes, here's what this old

ambassador has come to,
filching metaphors from the
firmament, only to get

lost in the ordinary,
the jewelry box, the socks
piled on the floor as if they

might, in time, walk to the
laundry room by themselves.
Oh, these papers, how wild they've

become, driven mad by the
way I brush against them, as
I cross the room corner to

corner, never resting, like
the reproach of a stuck
window, seething like slow

traffic in a southbound lane.
All I know is, those pages are
my Pile of Want. It wants to

be a novel, it wants to
tell of two men loving through
decades of turbulent gay

history in the heart of
the heart of the country...
Next to the Pile, a powder-

blue portable typewriter,
perhaps the last of its kind,
and two reams of paper, a

pile of boxed ribbons, the kind
that are black on top, red on
the bottom, did anyone

use the red part that much...
Yes, yes! Southbound lane, I hear
you! *Horn blows, driver might,* as

we used to say. I came by
it honestly, as most queers do.
Rather have a male organ

in my hand than a chocolate
bar, and that's saying something.
You and I, love, came to each

other from our corners of
shame, toweled down and pumped up,
desperate for a KO.

For thirty-nine years
I loved you so.

II.

The last tenants used toothpaste
to hide nail holes in the walls,
an old college-dorm trick.

I spot these impastos from
time to time, and resist the
urge to lick one. No horns sound

from below now, post-midnight
as silent as the past
flickering on its cramped screen.

You used to have to guess what
people were thinking. Not
anymore. Each night at this

time I get on the Internet
and read old reviews of this
building. Here's a One-Star

complaint: *During my time at
the Ambassador there was
never any hot water and*

*the mangement's failure to
provide a refrigerator
forced my self to live subhuman*

*followed by the fact that the
propertity manger
refused to provide a*

*simple A/C unit in
the summer, however they
put one in the so-called*

office and there complete
disregard in keeping this
building secured and even

spending a little tax
increment financing
money on a simple

secured access system is
a major issue in a
neighborhood where crime runs

ramped. DO NOT LIVE there, if
you do get out NOW After
I moved out I leanred that

due to the propertity
manger not providing
A/C window units a

elderly resident died
due to heat exposure so
that's what you've got to look

forward to living in the
Ambassador. If you choose
to live there after all this

I will add if your Gay or
Lesbian Bisexual
or Trans, do not tell them.

You will get kicked out before
you can unpack…

Now I have to stress these
reviews were written years
ago, prior to the

revolution, I mean
renovation. See how
spotless and neat this place is,

fresh paint on the doorknobs, new
carpets, new fridge, oven…
See my shoes? Don't my shoes look

happy, lined up against the
wall like they've got someplace to
go? Well, they could walk south,

past the Uptown Theater, grab
a smoke, grab a tattoo, sell
some plasma. Over on Main,

the hookers don't hang out like
they used to. They've found other
places to go, or maybe

jobs on the Internet,
degrees from those online
universities named for

cities, or states, or the Grand
Canyon. Say, do streets have
souls, and do the souls have a

place to go when the asphalt
crumbles? Or do streets just
grow weary, wish they could do

something besides point north and
south, or east and west? Maybe
my shoes could walk north next time,

past the stone lions of
Kansas City Life, Veterans
of Foreign Wars, the Voc-Tech

school, the office building at
31st Street. It's all
downhill from there to Penn

Valley Park—and what a sweet
spot that was, once upon a
time. Even now the parking

lot at the Museum has
a sign: HEAD-IN PARKING
ONLY. How do parents

explain that sign to their
children? I guess they say,
"Honey, this used to be a

place where men used to park,
in what I guess would be called
a HEAD-OUT PARKING kind

of way, so they could watch
other men drive by. And when
they saw a man they liked, why,

they'd flash their lights or pretend
to adjust their side view...
What's that, honey? You want me

to get to the part that comes
next? Well, you are not *going*
to know what happened next,

mister! You've been curious
enough for one day! Now do
you want to go to the

museum and see the big
cannons or not? Because we
could just turn right back around...."

Yes, it's a Midwestern town,
it has a *you-gotta-be-
kidding* kind of way with the

gays: *It's getting late. You men
should pick yourselves up and go
home.... Home. No, Home. A real* Home.

A *decent* Home. *A Home you
don't emerge from again. Not
ever. Please. Not in our*

lifetimes. Yes, love, we lived
unwelcome lives, you and
I, and learned to be grateful,

like the dog that barely
escapes the kick to the curb.
"You and me, you and me," like

the Randy Newman song, "You
and me, baby, you and me,
you and me, you and me,

baby...." Say, did we know one
of us would die first, like we
know some things and either take

them on the chin or go mad?
Things not spoken of, lest they
come true? Pieces of some pact

with the universe we hope
to re-negotiate
sometime in our lives, and don't

think about, and call that wise?

III

More often than not, when I
walk down the street with a smile
for everyone I see—

I get cut dead. It doesn't
matter. So the old grizzly
with yellow teeth isn't worth

looking at. I give myself
points for trying. Take this
sunny day: I made the

effort to get out, and now
I've got all the time in the
world to take in this blue bowl

of sky. As usual,
every cloud looks like a
penis. A thunderhead,

even, *head* being the
operative—wait. *Why* am
I facing the sky? And why—

I was going to say why
can't I hear, but sounds filter
in...like when you're lying on

the beach, trying to nap...
voices rise above the
breakers, buzzing, complaining...

like these voices rising now,
barely, over the breakers
of...passing cars. And one voice

calls out, closer than others:
"Hey, Pops!" Now if there's one thing
I hate... Pops ain't a person,

it's a concert, where you're forced
to listen to strings playing
"Raindrops Keep Fallin' on My

Head" till you want to cut your
wrists. *"Hey. Old Timer!"* Now, "Old
Timer" is better than "Pops,"

slightly. But if I can't see
where you're calling from, you're
of no use to me—no more

Than those bygone voices
at the beach. I need to
close my eyes now, and give

them a rest, anyway. But
wait: if I'm facing the sky,
then I…must be on my back?

Sure enough, if I stir my
shoulders—there's a cold hard
something. Sidewalk? And you there—

you who called to me—is that
your head obscuring the sky,
with its fast-moving dicks? *"He's*

alive," comes that voice again,
sounding as if he, like me,
can't tell if that's good news or

bad. Oh, I've been had by death
before, diddled on the cusp
between life and the very

same, frustrated, unfulfilled—
nothing to see here, folks. On
one occasion you, my love,

were there to hold my hand. It
was hard, not being able
to talk to you. Or was that

an ongoing theme throughout
our marriage? Real chatterbox,
wasn't I? Wrote a lot of

words, too. Made my living that
way. Yet often when we were
together...not much to say.

Shy? Struck dumb by love? Could it
be I didn't care enough?
Darling, if I could hold your

hand now.... Ah, no use fishing
in empty waters. What
happens when they all flush

away? Does even God know?
He's only had a trillion
billion years to think about

it, that's not long in God-time.
Now you, there, Oscar—the name
I've come up with for the grouch

with the voice—what do you think
of our current dilemma?
"Man, I ain't got time for this!"

Hey, I know that nasal whine.
Haven't I seen you around?
Don't you often spit in my

general direction? Ain't
it funny that because you
stopped and bent over me, you're

now obligated to care
for me for the rest of
my days? Ha ha, just kidding.

"I ain't got all day." Murmurs
of agreement surround him.
It's true, Oscar and friends don't

have all day to tend to me.
They have many hours to spend
hanging out by the plasma

center, doing nothing. And
keeping vigil over a
corpse isn't nothing. *"Hang on, Old*

Timer. Hang on, Old Man." Did
I close my eyes? Who said "corpse"?
Such a tidy word, like a

coin purse snapping shut. Penny?
Pen, Penny-O… I wish you
were here, I'd hate not to see

you again: a survivor,
as I have been. So young you
were, hair not quite the shade of

a new coin, green eyes, always
a buttoned-up cardigan,
dodging the dirty old men

who once roamed the hallways of
the old Ambassador. You've
seen the place at its worst and

then the rebirth. You, a
nursing student at the
Voc-Tech school when you moved

in, a teenager among
a few other students and
the aforementioned dirty

old men. You befriended one,
Old Man McCormack, to
your everlasting regret.

Then, when I moved in, you and
I became friends. You're still
my best friend in the building.

Okay, my only friend. We do
what loved ones do, make each other
necessary. Just as my

husband of many years made
me necessary, in a

world that couldn't tell what I
was good for. Perhaps he's here
now, gently tugging at me.

Darling, I've got so much to
tell you. They took down the
weeping willow in Loose Park,

the one you loved, that stood on
an island in the duck pond,
all by itself—no wonder

it wept. And they closed the
pizza place on Oak. It's been
forever, yet I can still

taste the sauce.... now the murmurs
rise in pitch, excitement stirs
the air. *Whoop* goes a siren.

Oscar's leaving, I'm sure those
are his steps quickening
toward the plasma center.

Strangers are taking over,
silhouettes blocking the sun.
Odd, how quickly I can be

secured and moved. Odder still,
I never thought till now—what
happened to me? Stroke, heart

attack, accident? Can I
talk? Should I try? Can I
even move on my own? What

have I lost? For this unwanted
nap on stone—what's the cost?

IV

Each day I'm wowed by the
surfaces around me. Smooth,
bright, cool to the touch. They soothe

me, prove I'm here, I've lasted,
even as they whisper to
each other, *We'll outlive the*

bastard. And these walls! So white,
so upright! Great for hanging
photos! Everybody does

it, everybody's got a
regular gallery in
their room. But I don't. Did I

misplace the past? Surely I
have one. Save me, bare walls.
You too, bare floors, with your

separate mission: keep me
in an upright position.
Gal down the hall slipped, broke her

hip in a million.... Penny
told me. Penny, the nursing
student who used to live at

the Ambassador, she's a
nurse now, dressed in all white.
Smooths out her sharp edges like

a blanket of snow. Now you,
my love, wouldn't recognize
me, zipping down the halls

like an old rolling pin,
rushing to fit in, maybe
joining a whole gang belting

out the old songs around a
donated piano, or
sunning ourselves on the cracked

patio, sitting so still
we could be… then a breeze comes
to stir a few wisps of hair

on the back of my neck, a
reminder I'm still living….
Yes! You bet! And still hungry,

tucking in at breakfast, lunch,
dinner, same place, same wobbly
table. Never missed a meal

in my life. Only once a
month the routine varies, on
Swedish Meatball Night. Then

I skip the dining room, and
Penny, giggling, smuggles
KFC down to my room.

We sit on my bed like kids
conspiring in a tent. I
tell her fried chicken isn't

bad for you if it's only
initials. Besides, I've
lost so much in recent times,

weight that is, I'm not even
sure it's me as I wheel down
the hall, looking at my thin

legs. I've lost so much, I want
to tell her, but not to fret,
KFC will survive,

even when there's no more
chicken, and no one left to
fry it. Why not. Why can't there

be something left. O husband,
thirty-nine years we had,
nothing left of us now but

me, and when I go...our
story will be gone. The sense
of it, if it had any,

the tender words, the laughter
no one else ever heard....
Penny takes my hand, holds it

as if it's still warm. She lost
something too when old man
McCormack died, in a room two

floors below hers at the old
Ambassador. She'd looked in
on him from time to time, changed

a light bulb, swept the floor,
till he mouthed off one day, and
she vowed she'd never look in

again. It was summer, a
brutal one, and old Mac
without a window unit....

They found him a month later,
Suffocated in his
armchair. Suffocated

and ripened for weeks. They did
their best, which wasn't much, to
clean the place up for a new

tenant, but they could never
quite get rid of the smell left
behind, a faint....*sweetish* smell.

Not a good kind of sweet, but
the hot breath of decay, and
once it got into your nose,

it never left. Somebody—
some college kid—took the place,
none the wiser. They didn't

even replace the armchair,
just sprayed it with stuff. A
lot of stuff. That was the old

Ambassador—they could
never do enough, so they
didn't even try. Now

Penny knows why, when others
might not—why I can't stand the
smell of those meatballs. *Sweetish*

meatballs. Oh Penny, don't blame
yourself over old Mac, he
sent you away, it wasn't

your fault. Maybe she feels
better when I say that, or
maybe not. At least a smile

tugs at her lips. "You're a
meatball," she says, only to
ask a moment later, "Are

you lonely?" I tell her I've
got stuff to keep me busy.
Memories, blank photo wall,

and—Yes!—the Pile of Want, set
up with typewriter, reams of
paper, ribbons, all on the

table by the window where
the last rays of the setting
sun drop in each night. How like

a museum exhibit,
remote, untouchable, prey
to the passage of time, which

used to be invisible
but seeps into the edges of
my vision like white vapor.

How about morning? Cup of
coffee, cup of tea. Look at
me, among all these shiny

surfaces, renewed every
day by the cleaning ladies.
They wear uniforms too, green

ones. "How are you today,
Mr. C.?" They can't deal with
my last name, and why should they—

I might not live long enough
for them to learn to pronounce
it. And that morning nurse,

Lucas—one of the most
joyous sights on earth, a Black
man in a white uniform.

What is loneliness? A
saxophone solo I used
to be able to play in

my head? A jazz step with no
partner? Hey hey, goin' to
Kansas City. 18th &

Vine. Stout black men with their
women and cigars, wreathed in
smoke and the most inspired

music of their time…. Told you
I wrote a lot of words. Now
what? Evening again? Seems like

it comes every day. In the
common room, a TV show
about a Chicago

hospital. Or Chicago
Fire Department. Everything
happens in Chicago.

Stories are all the same: folks
are mean, or they're kind. Or they
start out mean, then they're kind.

I didn't value kindness
when I didn't need it. You
don't value asparagus

if you don't eat it…. My love,
you were kind. I recall a
Saturday night at the

supermarket, we weaved our
way down a crowded aisle,
only to have a can of

hearts of palm roll across the
linoleum and lodge
against the wheel of our cart.

I tried to retrieve it, but
the elderly gal who had
dropped it got there first: "Oh, I'm

sorry," she said, "I'm so
sorry." "That's okay," you said.
"We're all in this together."

It was spring. You wore a
baseball cap, not typical
of you, but it gave you a

pleasing, sporty look. And on
future occasions you spoke
the same words, always at the

supermarket, which could be
counted on for awkward
situations: "We're all in

this together," you'd say, with
the same kind smile. And I
never asked where that saying

came from. How does a person
become so offhandedly
human, unthinkingly warm?

It must take more than years,
because I've had plenty of
those. Oh, my love, my sweetheart…!

Penny? Penny? I'm sorry,
it's nothing, I just reached my
hand out—I don't know why—and

scared myself, it's so wrinkled
and blue, cramped and cold, more like
a claw than a hand, perhaps

one of Prufrock's ragged claws
scuttling across the seabed....
No, no, I'm fine! It's my

education, you see, the
twentieth-century kind,
how quaint it seems now.

I remember.... Oh, thank you,
that's better. A warm blanket
doesn't solve everything, but

it solves most things. Yes, up to
my neck, please. I suppose, at
the end, the blanket—or sheet—

will be pulled up over my
face. I wonder...Before it
all scatters, will I see that

blue bowl of sky again? And
will a few clouds pass, smooth
and...erect? And you, my love,

my one and only, will you
be there? Can we hold hands, like
we did at the movies, in

the dark, so no one could see?
Or will they even care in eternity?
Will we be free? Will we be free?

Wayne Courtois was born in Maine and currently lives in Kansas City, Missouri with his husband of 34 years, Ralph Seligman. Wayne writes fiction, nonfiction, and poetry. He holds an MFA from the Writing Program at the University of

North Carolina-Greensboro, where he studied with Fred Chappell, and was awarded fellowships at the Cummington Community of the Arts and the Virginia Center for the Creative Arts. In Kansas City he served two terms as a board member of The Writers Place, and still serves on its Program Committee.

Short stories have appeared in: *The Greensboro Review, suspect thoughts: a journal of subversive writing, Velvet Mafia, Harrington Gay Men's Literary Journal, Best Gay Erotica 2005, Jonathan.* Novels: *My Name Is Rand* (Suspect Thoughts Press, 2004), *Tales My Body Told Me* (Lethe Press, 2010), *In the Time of Solution 9* (Lethe Press, 2013). *Memoir: A Report from Winter* (Lethe Press, 2009). Poetry Journals: *Chelsea Station Magazine, Assaracus, I-70 Review.* Poetry Anthologies: *Hibernation: Poems by Bear Bards, Gimme Your Lunch Money, The Shining Years.* Essays: *I Do/I Don't: Queers on Marriage; Walking Higher: Gay Men Write about the Deaths of Their Mothers; The Lost Library: Gay Fiction Rediscovered.*